Cooking
IN THE
HOUSE
OF
CASH

Cooking
IN THE
HOUSE
OF
CASH

Peggy Knight

PREMIUM PRESS AMERICA
NASHVILLE, TENNESSEE

Cooking in the House of Cash by Peggy Knight

Published by PREMIUM PRESS AMERICA

ISBN 1-887-654-93-3
Library of Congress Catalog Number 2004105842

PREMIUM PRESS AMERICA gift books are available at special discounts for premiums, sales promotions, fund-raising, or educational use. For details contact the Publisher at P.O. Box 159015, Nashville, TN 37215, or phone toll free (800) 891-7323 or (615) 256-8484, or fax (615) 256-8624.

www.premiumpressamerica.com

Design by Armour&Armour, Nashville, Tennessee

First Edition 2004

1 2 3 4 5 6 7 8 9 10

To my brother Alfred and my sisters
Shirley, Betty, Frances, and Juanita

CONTENTS

Carter and Cash Family Recipes

Foreword

Peggy Knight has traveled the world. The sights, scenes, customs, and tastes were experienced in her travels with Johnny and June Cash.

Peggy and Johnny and June Carter Cash hosted hundreds of parties, receptions, weddings, and get-togethers. She knows what lights up one's taste buds.

From her years of travel around the world, and hosting everyone from down-and-out musicians to kings and queens, Peggy has assembled this cookbook of her favorite recipes. I can hardly wait to put Peggy's cookbook to use in my home.

Duane Allen

Oak Ridge Boys

Maybelle, June, and John were real country people who favored country cooking—country ham and biscuits for breakfast, and vegetables and cornbread for dinner. They weren't hard to please.

That worked for me because before I went to work for Maybelle, I hadn't spent much time in a kitchen. But I did most of the cooking after I started staying with June and John in 1989. June loved to cook and collected a lot of recipes from family and friends.

June and John invited their friends from all walks of life to eat with us, especially for country ham breakfasts. Bob Duvall, John Schneider, Rodney Crowell, Kris Kristofferson, and Marty Stuart were just a few of our frequent guests. Before June and John got sick, we'd have parties for up to two hundred fifty people.

And like country people everywhere, they always insisted that drop-in visitors stay to eat. I just added to what I was cooking and we always seemed to have enough.

These recipes from Maybelle and June (and one from John for chili, the only thing I ever knew him to cook) provide a sampling of their special brand of hospitality. I've also included recipes for the favorite foods I fixed for them and their friends.

Add a little music from the Carter Family or Johnny Cash and enjoy.

—Peggy Knight

Breads

AUNT LOIS'S BANANA NUT BREAD

1½ cups Martha White All-Purpose Flour
¾ teaspoon soda
¼ teaspoon salt
1 cup sugar
2 eggs, slightly beaten
¾ cup oil
3 tablespoons buttermilk
2 to 3 bananas, mashed (about 1 cup)
½ cup chopped pecans

Preheat oven to 325 degrees. Grease and flour an 8½x4½x2½ inch loaf pan; set aside. Sift together flour, soda, and salt. Add sugar, eggs, oil, and buttermilk and stir to blend. Fold in bananas and nuts. Pour into prepared pan. Bake 1 hour 10 minutes, or until toothpick inserted in center comes out clean. Let cool in pan 15 minutes.

Turn out onto wire rack to cool completely. Makes 1 loaf.

Goodness gracious, it's good—just like the Carter family used to sing in the commercials for Martha White Flour. June got this recipe from "Aunt Lois," a cousin on Maybelle's side of the family.

PEGGY'S HOMEMADE BISCUITS

3 cups self-rising flour
½ cup shortening
2 cups buttermilk

John Jackson Routh, Carlene's son, loves my biscuits. When he was about seven years old, his family came down to Florida to stay a few days with us. When they were fixing to leave the house for the airport, he told June, "Grandma, I'll never see another biscuit as long as I live." Well, I went back inside and put some biscuits in a plastic bag. He snacked on them all the way back to Los Angeles. To this day, he calls me "Biscuit."

Cut shortening into flour with pastry blender, fork, or fingers. Add buttermilk and mix well. Sprinkle flour on piece of wax paper. Place dough on wax paper; knead slightly. Sprinkle small amount of flour on top of dough; roll out to about ¼ inch thick. Cut with a biscuit cutter, dipping it in flour after you cut each one. Place on a well-greased pan, rolling the biscuit over to grease the top side. Bake at 450 degrees about 10 minutes, until golden brown. Serve hot.

Makes 3 dozen.

Breads

BUTTERMILK PANCAKES

1 cup all purpose flour
1 tablespoon sugar
2 teaspoons baking powder
½ teaspoon baking soda
½ teaspoon salt
1¼ cups buttermilk
1 egg, slightly beaten
2 tablespoons vegetable oil
Syrup, warmed
Butter, melted

Blend together the dry ingredients. In a separate bowl, mix together the buttermilk, eggs, and oil. Add to dry ingredients, stirring lightly. (Batter should be lumpy.)

Spoon onto well-greased griddle or fry pan and cook until holes show through on top. Flip and brown other side. Serve with butter and syrup. Can serve with sausage or bacon and grits.

Makes about 12 pancakes.

Fresh strawberries are mighty good with pancakes, and Tennessee has the best strawberries in the world. Sometimes I'd fix bacon or grits to go with them, but June and John liked them just plain, too.

BRAN MUFFINS

¾ cup flour

¼ cup whole wheat flour

1 cup bran flakes

⅓ cup pecans

⅓ cup brown sugar

1 egg

¼ cup applesauce

¾ cup milk

¼ cup vegetable oil

1½ tablespoons sugar

½ cup raisins

Dash cinnamon

Preheat oven to 375 degrees. Combine all ingredients. Mix just until blended. Grease 2-inch muffin tins or line with paper cups. Fill ⅔ full. Bake 15 to 20 minutes or until brown.

Makes about 1 dozen 2-inch muffins.

I made a lot of bran muffins over the years. We'd have them for breakfast when we weren't having ham or bacon and eggs. They made great snacks, too. I'd just leave the muffins sitting out and pretty soon they were all gone.

PEGGY'S FAMOUS CORNBREAD

2 cups self-rising cornmeal
½ cup self-rising flour
1 egg, beaten
2 cups buttermilk
1 tablespoon sugar
⅔ cup oil

June and John would take hot cornbread right out of the skillet. They'd put some butter on it, crumble it in sweet milk or buttermilk, and eat like an appetizer before supper. For a night-time snack, June crumbled cold cornbread in sweet milk while John liked his cornbread in buttermilk.

Preheat oven to 450 degrees. Mix cornmeal, flour, egg, buttermilk, and sugar. Heat ⅓ cup oil in 12-inch iron skillet on stove top. Sprinkle some cornmeal in skillet. Pour in corn bread mixture and bake 20 minutes.

CORN PONE

2 cups plain cornmeal
½ teaspoon salt
1 teaspoon baking powder
1 tablespoon lard (shortening)
Milk

Corn pone is cornbread that you shape into small ovals—called pones in the South—with your hands and bake.

Preheat oven to 450 degrees.

Mix together cornmeal, baking powder, and salt; cut in lard; add milk to make a stiff batter. Form into pones with hands or drop with spoon in greased iron skillet. Bake for 30 minutes.

Makes 10 to 12.

CORN CAKES

2 cups plain cornmeal
1 tablespoon flour
2 eggs, beaten
1 teaspoon salt
2 teaspoons baking powder
1 tablespoon lard (shortening), melted
Milk

Mix together all ingredients, adding enough milk to make a medium thick batter. Spoon batter onto hot greased skillet. Cook on top of stove, turning to brown both sides.

Makes 10 to 12.

Cornbread should always be cooked in an iron skillet that you never use for anything else because it'll make the bread stick.

Iron skillets have to be properly seasoned and cared for. To season a new skillet, brush heavily with oil and bake in a slow oven for three or four hours.

Never wash an iron skillet in soapy water. Rinse with hot water and wipe clean with paper towel or cloth.

If your skillet gets rusty, build a fire outside and lay the skillet over the coals until the rust burns off.

ANNA BISCEGLIA'S EASTER BREAD

Anna used the green and blue eggs from the Araucana chickens we raised at the Cash compound to decorate her Easter bread. She made about twenty of these every Easter for us and her children and grandchildren. The Bisceglias worked for June and John for more than thirty years—she was the housekeeper and her husband Armond was a security guard.

4 boiled eggs, whole
½ cup vinegar
½ cup Romano cheese, cubed
½ cup Parmesan cheese, cubed
½ cup salami, cubed
½ cup pepperoni, cubed
3 boiled eggs, cubed
1½ tablespoons dry yeast
2 tablespoons warm water
1½ tablespoons Crisco (solid)
2 cups hot water
2 cups self-rising flour

In small pan, boil 7 eggs in water with ½ cup vinegar for 10 minutes. Keep 4 eggs in shells. Set aside to cool.

Dissolve yeast in warm water.

In mixing bowl, combine Romano and Parmesan cheeses, salami, pepperoni, and boiled eggs. Set aside.

In large bowl melt Crisco in hot water; add flour, stirring until blended. Add yeast mixture. Cover with cloth and let rise for 15 to 20 minutes.

Stir down dough. On floured board, roll out dough into rectangle about ½ inch thick, reserving enough dough to make eight ½-inch strips about 6 inches long. Spread rectangle of dough with cheese mixture; roll up like jelly roll.

Lightly grease 8-inch round bundt pan with Crisco. Place roll of dough in pan, pinching ends together where they meet. Place 4 eggs boiled in vinegar in dough, spaced apart. Criss-cross two strips of dough over each egg. Press ends of strip into dough.

Cover with cloth and let rise 15 to 20 minutes.

Bake in preheated 350-degree oven 1 hour.

CRACKLIN' BREAD

2 cups plain cornmeal
2 teaspoons salt
1 teaspoon soda
½ teaspoon baking powder
1 cup buttermilk
½ cup cracklins

Cracklings—or cracklins as we call them in the South—are the crispy bits left over from rendering lard from the fat skinned from hogs when they're killed. Add them to cornbread for extra flavor.

Preheat oven to 450 degrees. Mix ingredients. If too dry, add hot water. Put in hot greased skillet sprinkled with meal. Bake about 20 minutes until brown.

QUICK ROLLS

5 cups self-rising flour
1 cup butter-flavored Crisco
½ cup sugar
2 tablespoons yeast
2 cups buttermilk

Turn oven on warm. Cut shortening into flour and set aside. Add sugar and yeast to buttermilk. Microwave 1 minute (long enough to take the chill off). Stir to dissolve yeast. Add buttermilk/yeast mixture to flour and shortening, and mix well. Turn out as much as is needed onto floured biscuit board.* Roll or pat to ½ inch thick. Cut with 2- or 3-inch biscuit cutter; fold in half. Put close together in greased pan. Let rise in warm oven until doubled in size. Bake at 425 degrees 15 to 20 minutes until brown.

*Any unused dough will keep in refrigerator one week. To bake, follow directions above.

I used my recipe for quick rolls because I never knew how many would be at our table at mealtime. I could mix it up and cook the rolls right then or put the dough in the refrigerator to take out as needed. We nearly always had homemade bread of some kind —rolls, cornbread, or biscuits—with our meals.

I first met Maybelle in 1967 playing bingo, and we became great friends.

SPOON ROLLS

1 package dry yeast
2 cups very warm water
1½ sticks margarine, melted
¼ cup sugar
1 egg, beaten
4 cups self-rising flour

Place yeast in 2 cups warm water. Melt butter; cream it with sugar in large bowl. Add beaten egg. Add dissolved yeast to creamed mixture. Add the flour and stir until well mixed. Place in air tight bowl and keep in refrigerator.

To bake, stir down, knead gently, drop by spoonfuls into well-greased 2½-inch muffin tin. Bake at 350 degrees about 20 minutes. Dough keeps several days.

Yields 2 dozen.

In my early years with Maybelle and then with June and John, I made spoon rolls quite often. It's still one of my favorite recipes.

SOURDOUGH STARTER

¾ cup sugar
1 cup warm water
3 heaping tablespoons instant
potatoes, dry

There was a time when making sourdough bread was all the rage. I don't remember who gave me the starter — and the recipe—for "friendship" bread, as we called it. It was very good for sandwiches, and since it made three loaves, handy to have in the freezer.

In a medium bowl, thoroughly mix all the ingredients. Cover with foil; make a hole about the size of a quarter in the foil for air. Let the covered bowl stand, unrefrigerated, until little bubbles form on the top of the mixture. (This may take several days, depending on the room temperature.) When bubbles form, put the covered bowl into the refrigerator for 3 to 5 days.

Take the starter out of the refrigerator and "feed" it. (Feeding is adding the same three ingredients above, in the same amounts.) Let it sit out for 8 to 12 hours. Put it back into the refrigerator for 3 to 5 days.

Take the starter out and feed again. Let it sit out for 8 to 12 hours. Take out 1 cup of starter to use in making bread. Return the remaining starter to the refrigerator for 3 to 5 days.

Remove to feed again. Let stand for 8 to 12 hours. If not making bread after this feeding, throw away 1 cup of starter or give it to a friend or neighbor. The starter must be fed every 3 to 5 days.

SOURDOUGH BREAD

6 cups all-purpose flour
½ cup sugar
1 tablespoon salt
1½ cups warm water
½ cup oil
1 cup Sourdough Starter (page 18)

In a large bowl, mix all the ingredients together to make a stiff batter. Grease another large bowl. Put the dough in the greased bowl and brush the top of the dough with oil; cover lightly with foil and let set overnight. (Do not refrigerate.) Next morning, punch down the dough and knead it a little. Divide the dough into three parts; knead each part a little. Put each part into a greased loaf pan. Let rise until the dough reaches the top of the pan. (This may take all day since it rises slowly.) Bake at 350 degrees for 30 to 35 minutes. Remove from pans and cool on a rack. Wrap or put into plastic bags.

Makes 3 loaves.

NOTE: This bread freezes well.

For whole wheat bread: use 4½ cups bread flour and 1½ cups whole wheat flour. All other ingredients as above. Bake as directed for white bread.

HUSH PUPPIES

3 cups self-rising cornmeal
1 tablespoon garlic powder
1 large onion, chopped fine
2 to 3 cups buttermilk
Mazola or Crisco oil
(can use same oil used to fry fish on
page 120)

Ruth and Billy Graham visited us often in Florida and in Hendersonville. Ruth loved to cook and was a lot of help to me in the kitchen. Many times she'd already have the coffee made when I got up.

Mix cornmeal, garlic powder, and onion until well blended. Add enough buttermilk slowly to form a batter thick enough to drop from a spoon. Dip tablespoon in batter and drop into hot oil (about 3 inches deep) in a deep fat fryer or deep iron skillet or pan. Fry to golden brown and drain on absorbent paper.

Soups, Salads, Dressings

CUCUMBER SOUP

6 big cucumbers
1 cup half-and-half
Salt and pepper to taste
⅛ teaspoon garlic powder
½ teaspoon cream of tartar
⅓ stick butter

Peel and slice cucumbers. Put in pan with small amount of water. Cook until tender. Drain, put in blender with half-and-half, salt, pepper, garlic powder, and cream of tartar. Blend until smooth. Transfer to pan on stove. Add ⅓ stick butter, and simmer for 10 minutes.

John ate this cucumber soup like crazy. But he wouldn't touch a cucumber in a salad with a ten-foot pole.

CHICKEN CORN SOUP

1 whole chicken or chicken pieces
2 onions, chopped
2 stalks celery, chopped
2 potatoes, chopped
3 large carrots, chopped
2 cans whole kernel corn
½ stick butter
Salt and pepper to taste

Cover whole chicken or chicken pieces with water and boil until tender. Remove chicken from broth and pick meat off bones. Return chicken pieces to broth. Add cut-up celery, onions, potatoes, carrots, corn, butter, salt, and pepper. Simmer until done.

Serves 8 to 10.

The good thing about this soup is we could cook it on the bus when we were on tour. June or I would put it on in the morning and and let it simmer. We'd have a good hot lunch or early supper before we got to the next town for our performance.

TOMATO SOUP

5 or 6 fresh tomatoes
OR 2 large cans Ro-Tel tomatoes
½ teaspoon sugar
Salt and pepper to taste

This was one of our favorite soups, whether we were at home, in Jamaica, or on the bus touring the countryside.

Cook tomatoes until tender. Blend in blender until creamy. Put tomatoes back in pot and add sugar, salt, and pepper. If not thick enough, add 1 tablespoon cornstarch or flour mixed with 2 tablespoons water. Simmer until hot.

VEGETABLE SOUP

4 potatoes, chopped
1 large onion, chopped
2 stalks celery, chopped
3 large carrots, sliced
Leftover roast beef

We mostly made vegetable soup in the winter when we were in Florida or Jamaica. Sometimes we would also have a sandwich with this soup for lunch.

Put potatoes, onion, celery, and carrots in soup pot. Add just enough water to cover vegetables. Bring to boil. Add leftover roast beef, and salt and pepper to taste. Simmer until vegetables are tender.

BROCCOLI/ CAULIFLOWER SALAD

Salad:

2 bunches broccoli

1 head cauliflower

1 small red onion, chopped

1 cup cheddar cheese, grated

½ pound bacon
   (cooked crisp and crumbled)

Cut broccoli and cauliflower into bite-sized pieces. Combine all ingredients and mix well.

Dressing:

½ cup mayonnaise

½ cup sugar

¼ cup vinegar

¼ cup oil

Combine mayonnaise, sugar, vinegar, and oil. Pour over salad mixture. Mix well. Delicious!

Everybody loved this delicious salad but John, who couldn't stand broccoli or cauliflower.

CITRUS AVOCADO SALAD

Salad:
Mixed greens
1 avocado, sliced
1 can mandarin oranges, drained
1 red onion, slivered
½ cup almonds, chopped

Dressing:
¼ cup orange juice
¼ cup lime juice
4 tablespoons olive oil
2 tablespoons honey
2 tablespoons balsamic vinegar
1 teaspoon Dijon mustard
¼ teaspoon black pepper
½ teaspoon salt
½ teaspoon oregano

Combine dressing ingredients until well blended. Pour over salad mixture. Toss well.

Johnny Cash embraces an emotional Maybelle at the Grand Ole Opry's last night at the Ryman Auditorium.

JUNE'S FRUIT SALAD

1 can peach pie filling
1 large can mandarin oranges
1 large can pineapple tidbits
1 container frozen strawberries
1 or 2 bananas, sliced

Lunch for June, John, and me was usually soup, salad, a sandwich, or any combination of these. A BLT was our favorite, especially in the summer. June's fruit salad was a quickie when we didn't have much time.

Drain mandarin oranges and pineapple. Combine ingredients and add sliced bananas at the last minute.

GORGONZOLA AND WALNUT SALAD

Salad:
Mixed greens
½ pound gorgonzola
1 cup chopped walnuts
1 Red Delicious apple or pomegranate,
chopped

Dressing:
1 tablespoon Dijon mustard
4 tablespoons wine vinegar
1 tablespoon lemon juice
½ cup walnut oil
½ teaspoon salt
¼ teaspoon pepper

Mix together dressing ingredients until
well blended. Pour over salad mixture.
Toss well.

POTATO SALAD

2½ pounds red potatoes
1½ bunches of green onions, including tops
1 large jar pimento, drained
4 boiled eggs
2 stalks celery
5 kosher dill pickles
1 teaspoon sugar
1 cup Miracle Whip salad dressing
1 tablespoon mustard
Salt and pepper
Paprika

The red potatoes add color to this basic recipe for potato salad. It's good with vegetables or sandwiches.

Scrub potatoes; you may leave the peel on for color. Boil until fork comes out easily. Cut into cubes when slightly cool, but still warm. Cut onions, pimento, eggs, celery, and pickles into cubes or pieces. Mix into potatoes with sugar, salad dressing, and mustard. Add salt and black pepper to taste. Sprinkle paprika on top. Chill before serving.

JUNE'S BAKED POTATO SALAD

8 medium potatoes, cooked and chopped
8 ounces American cheese, chopped
¼ cup chopped onion
¼ cup chopped celery
8 ounces bacon, crisp-fried, crumbled
1 cup mayonnaise
Salt and pepper to taste
1 cup Ritz cracker crumbs

I used June's recipe for potato salad when we wanted a hot dish to go with whatever else we were having for lunch or supper.

Combine potatoes, cheese, onion, celery, bacon, mayonnaise, salt, and pepper in bowl; mix well. Spoon into buttered 9x13-inch baking pan. Sprinkle Ritz cracker crumbs on top. Bake at 350 degrees for 55 minutes.

Serves 8 to 12.

CREAMY POTATO SALAD

8 to 10 white potatoes, peeled and
  chopped into ½-inch cubes
1 small jar sweet pickle relish
½ cup chopped celery
4 large boiled eggs, chopped
½ cup chopped apples
1 tablespoon mustard
1 tablespoon vinegar
1 tablespoon sugar
5 tablespoons mayonnaise
  (or enough to make creamy)
Salt and pepper to taste
Optional: 2 green onions, chopped

This is the potato salad June and John liked best. We cooked it mostly when we were having company.

Boil potatoes with salt and pepper until soft. (Note: It is best to season the potatoes while cooking so the seasoning will go through the potatoes.) Drain well. Mix all ingredients while potatoes are hot. This will make a creamy potato salad. Suggestion: Try eating while hot.

Serves 8 to 10.

SPINACH SALAD

Salad:

Baby spinach leaves

1 pink grapefruit, sectioned and chopped

½ cup toasted pine nuts

½ cup dried currants

Dressing:

2 tablespoons red wine vinegar

2 teaspoons sugar

1 teaspoon coarse salt

6 tablespoons olive oil

Mix dressing until well blended. Pour over salad mixture and toss well.

We could just pull the grapefruits off the trees in our yard in Jamaica so we had this salad a lot.

MAYBELLE'S KILL THE LETTUCE

4 strips bacon
2 to 3 bunches leaf lettuce,
*   washed and drained*
8 to 10 green onions, sliced including tops
Hot bacon grease

Maybelle called this "Kill the Lettuce," but others referred to it as wilted lettuce. She liked it for any meal, particularly with green beans or pintos and potatoes.

Fry bacon until crisp. Crumble and set aside. Leave bacon drippings in skillet.

Tear lettuce into bits and place in bowl. Add green onions and toss. Add crumbled bacon; pour hot bacon grease over salad.

SPINACH AND STRAWBERRY SALAD

Salad:
Baby spinach leaves
Strawberries
Toasted almonds or pecans

Dressing:
¼ cup sugar
2 tablespoons sesame seeds
1½ teaspoons minced onion
½ teaspoon Worchestershire sauce
¼ teaspoon paprika
½ cup oil
½ cup vinegar

Mix dressing ingredients until well blended. Pour over salad mixture and toss well.

SPRINGTIME APRICOT SALAD

6-ounce package apricot Jello
⅔ cup boiling water
20-ounce can crushed pineapple
* (do not drain)*
8-ounce package regular cream cheese,
* cut into small cubes*
1 large tub Cool Whip
1 cup chopped pecans
Maraschino cherries

Leanne Abell, one of the nurses who took care of June and John many times when they were at Baptist Hospital, gave us this recipe. One time she and John got to talking about food. She said she loved to cook and had a lot of good recipes, including this one.

In large bowl, dissolve Jello in boiling water; add pineapple and juice. Stir to mix well. Stir cream cheese cubes into hot Jello mixture. (Cream cheese will melt into the mixture slightly.) Let cool to room temperature, then fold in the Cool Whip and pecans. Mix well. Pour into 9x13-inch dish and cool in refrigerator. Garnish with Maraschino cherries.

TEXAS SALAD

2 cans chili hot beans
2 hard boiled eggs, chopped
1 medium onion, chopped
1 large green pepper, chopped
2 or 3 tomatoes, cut up
1 package shredded cheddar
   or Mexican cheese
1 package corn chips
1 bottle Catalina dressing (chilled)

This was one of our favorite salads for lunch. But then John liked anything that in any way resembled chili. He liked hot stuff.

In large bowl, mix first six ingredients. Just before serving, add corn chips and just enough dressing to moisten all ingredients.

FRUIT SALAD DRESSING

1 cup corn oil
½ cup light corn syrup
⅓ cup vinegar
1 tablespoon grated onion
1 teaspoon salt
1 teaspoon dry mustard
1 teaspoon paprika
1 teaspoon celery seed

Combine all ingredients. Beat with rotary beater until well blended and thick. Place in covered container. Chill several hours. Shake thoroughly before serving.

For variety, substitute poppy seed or sesame seed for celery seed.

Makes about 1¾ cups.

We'd combine whatever fresh fruit we had on hand — apples, oranges, bananas, strawberries, grapes, pears, cherries—then add June's special dressing. I fixed it for lunch, or it was good as a simple dessert by itself or with other sweets.

JUNE'S HOT BACON DRESSING

1 slice bacon
2 tablespoons diced celery
3 tablespoons minced onion
3 tablespoons red wine vinegar
3 tablespoons apple cider vinegar
4 tablespoons firmly packed brown sugar
1 teaspoon whole-grain mustard
1 cup olive oil
Salt and pepper to taste

This recipe of June's was another of our favorite dressings for a tossed salad. It was just as good on a big luncheon salad as it was at dinner.

Cook bacon in skillet until crisp. Remove bacon and set aside. To skillet, add celery and onion. Cook for 2 minutes on medium heat or until tender. Add red wine vinegar, apple cider vinegar, brown sugar, whole-grain mustard, salt, and pepper. Simmer 10 minutes. Remove from heat. Slowly stir in 1 cup olive oil, blending to make an emulsion. Crumble bacon and add to dressing.

Makes 6 servings.

JUNE'S VINEGAR AND OIL DRESSING

½ cup oil
½ cup vinegar
3 tablespoons sugar
⅛ teaspoon garlic powder
Dash of salt

This simple recipe of June's goes well with all kinds of salads.

Mix all ingredients in a jar; cover and shake until well mixed. Pour over salad.

BETTY'S COLE SLAW

1 large head cabbage
4 carrots
½ cup vinegar
2 tablespoons sugar
½ cup mayonnaise

Shred cabbage and grate carrots until fine.
Add vinegar, sugar and mayonnaise and
mix well.

John always wanted my sister Betty to make coleslaw and hush puppies to go with the fish she cooked.

Vegetables
and
Casseroles

JUNE'S FRIED CABBAGE

1 head cabbage
½ stick butter
Sugar
Salt
Pepper

Wash and drain cabbage. Separate and cut up leaves slightly. Melt butter in skillet; add cabbage. Stir while cooking, about 10 minutes. Sprinkle with salt, pepper, and sugar.

June and John liked country cooking. It was just fine with them to have all vegetables and no meat. June particularly like fried cabbage, which she taught me how to cook. You can't cook it very long or else it will be soggy.

FRIED CORN

6 to 10 ears fresh Silver Queen corn
4 tablespoons butter

I'd freeze a lot of corn in the summer so we could have it year round. To freeze, prepare as for fried corn. Place corn in heavy pot, barely covering with water. Bring to heavy boil, then set off to cool completely. When cool, put in heavy freezer bags and place in freezer.

Remove the husks and silk from fresh ears of Silver Queen corn. Thinly slice the grains from the cob twice with a sharp knife. Then scrape the cob with the blunt side of the knife to get all the milky liquid.

Heat 4 tablespoons butter in skillet; add corn, salt, and pepper. Simmer until tender, stirring occasionally. If it doesn't thicken, mix 1 tablespoon self-rising flour with 2 tablespoons water and add to corn.

If using frozen corn, melt butter in skillet, add frozen corn, then salt and pepper and follow directions above.

CORNBREAD CASSEROLE

1½ pounds ground beef, browned
    and drained
1 small can chopped chilies
1 onion, chopped
1 package jalapeno cornbread mix
¾ cup milk
1 egg, beaten
1 can creamed corn
3 cups cheese, Monterey Jack
    and cheddar
¼ cup oil

Simmer drained ground beef, chilies, and onion about 10 minutes. Combine cornbread mix, milk, egg, and corn. Pour oil in large skillet and heat. Pour half of batter in skillet, then add beef mixture, and half of cheese. Add rest of batter and top with cheese. Cook 40 to 45 minutes at 400 degrees.

Serves 8 to 10.

Everybody needs more than one iron skillet. I never cooked this recipe in the skillet I used only for bread.

GRITS

2 cups boiling water
1 cup grits
Salt

We always had grits with our country ham breakfasts: when it was just us and especially when we had company. When I made red-eye gravy, we'd spoon it over the grits.

Stir grits into boiling water; add dash of salt. Cook about 5 minutes, stirring occasionally until it thickens. You may add milk, butter, or sugar or spoon red-eye gravy (see page 96) over the grits.

MACARONI AND CHEESE

8-ounce package elbow macaroni

2 tablespoons butter

3 cups cheese, grated (your choice)

1¼ cups milk, regular or
*   evaporated*

Salt and pepper to taste

¼ cup bread crumbs (optional)

Cook macaroni using package directions. Drain well. Place back into pot. Add butter to macaroni, stirring frequently until butter melts. Place half of macaroni in 8x11-inch baking dish. Spread with half of cheese. Repeat layer of macaroni and cheese. Pour milk over the entire dish. Sprinkle with salt, pepper, and bread crumbs. Bake 20 minutes at 350 degrees or until light brown and bubbly.

June and John liked my macaroni and cheese so well that I had two recipes, just so it wasn't always the same.

MACARONI AND CHEESE

1½ cups elbow macaroni
2 tablespoons butter
2 tablespoons all-purpose flour
½ teaspoon salt
2 cups milk
2 cups American cheese, grated

Marty Stuart, who played in John's band and was once married to Cindy Cash, always laughed about dropping in to visit just about the time we were sitting down to eat. We saw him a lot—especially after he bought the house next door.

Cook macaroni in boiling salt water. Do not overcook. Drain. In saucepan, blend butter, flour, salt, and then add milk. Cook over medium heat until mixture boils. Add cheese and macaroni. Fold into a 1½-quart baking dish. Bake uncovered for 30 minutes at 350 degrees.

MACARONI AND TOMATOES

1½ cups macaroni
1 large can tomatoes
½ stick margarine
Salt
Sugar

Cook macaroni according to package directions. Drain. Pour in a large can of tomatoes. Cook about 15 minutes. Add margarine and salt and sugar to taste.

This was one of June's favorite dishes. If there was any left over—and sometimes we made more just so there would be—we used it to make goulash. (See next page.)

JUNE'S GOULASH

1 pound ground beef
1 onion, chopped
1 green pepper, chopped
Leftover macaroni and tomatoes

I don't know where June got this recipe—she might have just made it up. Anyway it was another quick meal that I fixed a lot. With their busy schedules, it was not always possible to plan ahead.

Brown ground beef in skillet. Add onions, green pepper, leftover macaroni and tomatoes. Simmer 5 minutes.

PINEAPPLE CHEESE CASSEROLE

2 20-ounce cans of chunk pineapple
(drained)
1 cup grated cheddar cheese
⅔ cup sugar
1 tablespoon flour
1 stick butter, melted
24 Ritz crackers (crushed)

Spread pineapple in 9x13-inch baking dish. Mix cheese, flour, and sugar together; spread on pineapple. Spread crushed Ritz crackers on top of casserole; cover with melted butter. Bake at 325 degrees for 20 minutes.

This made a nice side dish for whatever we were having.

FRIED OKRA

1 pound okra
1 cup self-rising cornmeal
1 tablespoon self-rising flour
Mazola oil
Salt
Pepper

John loved fried foods. But after he discovered he had diabetes, I started using Mazola oil since it was healthier than other oils or shortenings.

Wash okra, slice crosswise. Combine cornmeal and flour and roll okra slices in mixture until well coated. Place in hot oil about ¼ inch deep in skillet, sprinkle with salt and pepper to taste. Cook in Mazola oil, turning once until brown on both sides.

Serves 4.

PINTO BEANS

1 cup dried pinto beans, washed
4 cups cool water
1 tablespoon salt
3 ounces salt pork or hog jowl

Both June and John loved pinto beans with cornbread. John would put pinto beans on his plate and top them with my homemade green tomato chow chow (page 183). June liked chopped onions with hers.

Bring beans to a full boil for 5 minutes, then cut heat down to simmer for one hour. Then cook on medium heat until tender, about 1½ hours. Serve with cornbread and onion or chow chow.

SHOE-PEG CORN/ GREEN BEAN CASSEROLE

1 can French style green beans
1 can shoe-peg corn
1 can sliced water chestnuts
½ cup onion, chopped
1 cup cheese, grated
1 cup sour cream
1 can cream of celery soup
1 stick butter, melted
1½ cup Ritz crackers, crushed

Layer the first five ingredients in order listed in buttered 8x11-inch casserole dish.

Mix sour cream and soup, and pour over casserole.

Add crushed Ritz crackers to melted butter. Spread on casserole. Bake at 350 degrees for 45 minutes or an hour.

This was one of June's specialties. She fixed it quite a bit, particularly when we were in Florida and Jamaica.

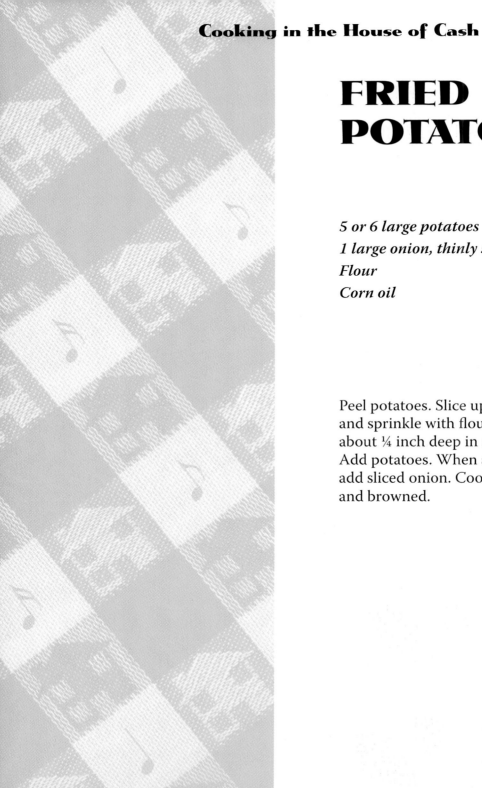

FRIED POTATOES

5 or 6 large potatoes
1 large onion, thinly sliced
Flour
Corn oil

Peel potatoes. Slice up and down, and sprinkle with flour. Pour oil about ¼ inch deep in skillet and heat. Add potatoes. When almost done, add sliced onion. Cook until tender and browned.

SQUASH CASSEROLE

5 or 6 cups squash (before cooking)
1 can cream of chicken soup
1 cup sour cream
1 large carrot, grated
1 small jar pimento
1 cup cheddar cheese, grated
1 medium onion, grated
1 stick margarine
Salt and pepper to taste
½ bag Pepperidge Farm
   seasoned bread crumbs

I often cooked this for June and John, especially in the summer. It is very tasty with other vegetables and sliced tomatoes.

Cook squash and drain. Add salt, pepper, and all other ingredients except bread crumbs. Spread half of bread crumbs on bottom of greased 9x13-inch casserole dish. Add squash mixture; top with remaining bread crumbs. Bake at 350 degrees for 1 hour.

JUNE'S SWEET POTATOES

6 medium sweet potatoes
½ cup orange juice
3 eggs, beaten
1 stick butter
1½ cups sugar
½ cup brown sugar
½ teaspoon nutmeg

Boil peeled sweet potatoes until tender. Mash and mix in remaining ingredients. Pour into greased 9x13-inch baking dish. Place topping over mixture.

Topping:
3 cups corn flakes
1 stick butter, softened
1 cup pecans

Mix corn flakes and pecans in soft butter and place on sweet potato mixture. Bake at 300 degrees for 15 minutes.

When we had sweet potatoes with our Thanksgiving dinner, we used this recipe of June's.

BAKED SWEET POTATOES

6 sweet potatoes
Wesson oil

Wash sweet potatoes and pat dry. Brush with Wesson oil. Place in shallow pan and bake at 350 degrees about 1 hour.

Serves 6.

John was particularly fond of baked sweet potatoes. They were both easy to cook and delicious.

ASPARAGUS WITH EGG AND WHITE SAUCE

2 cans asparagus spears
2 hard boiled eggs, diced
3 tablespoons butter
Salt
½ cup all-purpose flour
1⅛ cup whole milk

Heat and drain asparagus. Spray a heavy skillet with Pam, then melt butter and stir in the flour over low heat. Mix well, making sure to keep the mixture white. Add dash of salt and milk. Stir until mixture gets a little thick. Remove from heat. Place asparagus in a shallow dish; cover with diced eggs. Pour white sauce over all. Serve hot.

My friend Earlene Holt often made this for June and John or I would make it for them from her recipe. They also loved her homemade bread that she brought them from time to time.

Main Dishes
and Meats

BEEF ENCHILADAS

1 dozen corn tortillas
2 8-ounce cans enchilada sauce
1½ pounds ground beef, browned
*   and drained*
1 onion, chopped
1 can pitted olives
1 dash garlic powder
¾ pound grated cheese
3 tablespoons flour
3 tablespoons chili powder
15-ounce can refried beans
Oil, warmed (enough to dip tortillas)

This was easy to fix in the cramped kitchen of the tour bus when we were traveling. When we were on the road, we cooked for ourselves a lot—to save time, but also to have a home-cooked meal.

Dip tortilla in warm oil to soften, then dip in enchilada sauce. Put layer of ground beef, beans, cheese, onions, and olives on tortilla. Roll tortilla and place in 8½x11-inch pan or baking dish. Sprinkle remaining ground beef, cheese, onions, and olives on top of enchiladas; pour remaining enchilada sauce over all.

Bake 20 to 25 minutes. Serve immediately.

Serves 8.

MAYBELLE'S FRIED CHICKEN

1 whole frying chicken, cut up,
* or 4 chicken breasts*
1¼ cups flour
1½ teaspoons salt
1 teaspoon black pepper
1 cup buttermilk
1 cup oil

Wash chicken and pat dry with paper towels. Mix flour, salt, and pepper together in flat bowl. Dip chicken pieces in buttermilk then roll in the flour mixture until well coated. In large cast iron skillet, heat the oil on medium heat. Lay the pieces gently in hot oil, with space between them. Bring the heat to medium high until the chicken is golden brown. Turn chicken with tongs and brown other side. Turn the heat down to medium low, cover the skillet, and let cook for another 20 minutes. When done, place on absorbent paper towels to soak up excess grease.

Chicken may be put on platter and kept in warm oven until ready to serve.

I had been frying chicken for years before I started taking care of Maybelle. She taught me how she fried chicken and I've been frying it her way ever since. She always wanted to have fried chicken whenever her friends or kinfolks came over to eat with us. I fried a lot of chicken in that little kitchen on the tour bus, too. I always fry chicken in an iron skillet, but not in the one I use for cornbread.

CHICKEN GRAVY

Crumbs and drippings left in
  skillet after frying chicken
¼ cup flour
2 cups milk

Add flour to the crumbs in the skillet. Lightly brown the flour, then add 2 cups milk. Stir constantly until it thickens. Serve over hot biscuits.

BEEF TENDERLOIN

1 filet of beef, about 5 pounds
1 package McCormick's marinade for beef
Salt
Pepper
Garlic powder

Trim fat from tenderloin. Wash well and pat dry. Place in roasting pan just big enough to hold filet. Prick meat with fork. Mix marinade with enough water to cover tenderloin. Cover and marinate 3 to 4 hours in refrigerator, turning several times. Remove from pan and drain. Rub with salt, pepper, and garlic powder. Place on broiler pan. Bake 30 minutes in 450-degree oven. Broil for 3 to 5 minutes to brown. Let stand for 15 minutes before cutting tenderloin into ½-inch slices. Most of the tenderloin will be medium, with the thicker part medium rare and the tail medium well. Place on platter, decorate with parsley. Slice thinner if serving as hors d'oeuvres on rolls or biscuits.

Serves 10 to 12.

June always wanted to have this for any party we had. It was also good to have when folks dropped by and stayed to have dinner with us since it cooks in such a short time. We liked it better fresh than frozen so I would run to the store, cut down on the marinating time, and still have it ready for unexpected company.

JUNE'S CHICKEN ASPARAGUS AU GRATIN

4 cups soft bread, cubed
1 cup grated cheese
½ cup butter, melted
2 cups cooked asparagus
½ cup flour
3 cups milk
3 cups cooked chicken, diced
Salt and pepper to taste

Mix bread cubes, cheese, and half the butter. Spread half the bread mixture in greased 2-quart baking dish. Place asparagus on bread mixture. Blend flour, salt, pepper, and remaining butter in sauce pan; add milk. Cook, stirring until thick and smooth. Add chicken and pour over asparagus. Place remaining bread cubes on top. Bake at 350 degrees for 30 to 40 minutes.

Serves 8 to 10.

June mostly cooked this just for us; she never thought it was a dish for company.

CHICKEN SUPREME

4-pound hen or fryer
2 cans cream of mushroom soup
1 can chicken broth
3-ounce can chopped pimentos
½ cup celery, chopped
1 cup green peas, cooked
1 tablespoon finely chopped onions
3 hard-boiled eggs, sliced

In saucepan, cover chicken with water and boil until fork tender. Remove skin and bones, and cut meat into chunks. Combine soup and broth in saucepan, and heat. When hot, add chicken, then lightly fold in pimentos, celery, green peas, onions, and hard boiled eggs. Keep warm but do not overcook. Serve over cornbread (See page 8.)

Makes 8 generous servings.

June and John were not picky eaters. Mostly June would just say "Honey, fix what you feel like cookin' and we'll eat it."

CHICKEN AND DRESSING

12" skillet of cornbread
  (see cornbread recipe on page 10)
1 large onion, chopped
2 stalks celery, chopped
2 boiled eggs, chopped
Salt and pepper
2 teaspoons sage
Chicken or turkey broth

Sauté onions and celery. Crumble cornbread and mix all ingredients with enough broth to make it kind of soft, not dry. Taste mixture, and add more sage, pepper, or salt if needed. Put in a large pan and bake at 350 degrees for about 15 minutes. Make sure it doesn't dry out. If it does, add more broth to keep it real moist.

BAKED CHICKEN

4- to 5-pound hen or chicken
2 or 3 tablespoons butter, melted
Salt
Pepper
Garlic powder

Remove and discard giblets. Rinse chicken and pat dry with paper towels. Place chicken, breast side up, on greased rack of shallow roasting pan. Sprinkle with salt, pepper, and a little garlic powder. Brush with melted butter. Bake in a preheated 400-degree oven about 1 hour.

JOHN'S CHILI

Johm made this all the time—the only thing he ever cooked. He used plenty of chili powder and peppers, and it was so hot June couldn't eat it. Sometimes he would substitute deer meat for the sirloin.

5 pounds sirloin steak or deer meat
3 packages McCormick's, Schilling,
  Lawry's or any good chili seasoning mix
Mexene chili powder to taste
Spice Island chili con carne seasoning
1 tablespoon cumin
1 tablespoon thyme
6 sage leaves
2 large onions, chopped
6 chili peppers, chopped
3 or 4 cans red kidney beans
3 or 4 cans whole tomatoes
1 can tomato paste
Garlic powder to taste
Onion powder to taste
2 tablespoons sugar
Salt to taste

Chop steak and cook with a little shortening until medium. Add packages of chili seasoning mix and cook 5 minutes. Add beans, tomatoes, spices, onions, sugar, chili powder, and chili con carne mix. Taste. If chili is too hot for the children or ladies, add 1 or 2 cans of tomatoes. Add tomato paste. If it gets too thick, add water. Simmer on low heat for 20 minutes. Serve with soda crackers and Pepsi or Coke. This will serve 12 people, three helpings each.

To my Gal Peggy —
Thanks for the beautiful
smiles and wonderful food!

John Schneider

3-4-86

COUNTRY HAM

4 slices Harpers country ham
¼ cup oil
Sugar

Grease bottom of cast iron skillet with oil. Add ham and cook over medium heat for about 7 minutes per side. Just before it gets done, sprinkle a small amount of sugar on the slices. Heat for one minute more per side. Serve hot.

John Schneider, the Dukes of Hazzard star who is also a recording artist, loved anything I cooked, but a country ham breakfast was his favorite.

MILK GRAVY

¼ *cup oil*
6 to 7 tablespoons flour
¼ *teaspoon salt*
¼ *teaspoon black pepper*
2½ cups milk
½ *stick butter*

I'd make milk gravy for folks who didn't like red-eye. Some, of course, would eat both.

In a cast iron skillet, mix oil, flour, salt, and pepper. Cook until flour starts to brown. Add butter, then milk, and cook until the mixture gets thick. Serve hot.

RED-EYE GRAVY

¾ *cup ham drippings*
¼ *cup freshly brewed coffee*

Pour ham drippings from iron skillet into heavy bowl. Heat skillet until it is almost smoking and add coffee. Stir and pour into drippings. Mix and serve over hot biscuits.

MEXICAN CHICKEN

4 or 5 chicken breasts, boiled, deboned,
  and chopped
1 bag corn chips, crushed
1 can mushroom soup
1 can mild Ro-Tel tomatoes
1 package dry taco mix
4 or 5 ounces shredded cheese

Layer chicken and crushed chips in a greased 9x13-inch baking dish (enough chips to cover top of chicken). Mix all other ingredients except cheese. Pour over chicken and chips. Sprinkle with cheese and cover. Bake at 350 degrees for 20 to 25 minutes.

GLAZED HAM

2- to 3-pound canned ham
1 small can pineapple slices
1 small jar Maraschino cherries
½ to ¾ bottle LaChoy Sweet & Sour Sauce
½ cup brown sugar

This is one of the best baked ham recipes I've ever had, but I don't remember who gave it to me. I'd fix it for supper, and if there was any left, we'd have ham sandwiches for lunch.

Place ham in a roasting pan; secure pineapple on top and around sides of ham with toothpicks. Place Maraschino cherries in the center of each pineapple slice and secure with toothpicks.

Mix LaChoy Sweet & Sour Sauce and brown sugar to make a thin paste. Pour mixture over ham. Bake 1 hour at 450 degrees, basting occasionally with sauce.

HAMBURGER CASSEROLE

1 pound ground beef
½ pound sausage
1 large onion, chopped
8 ounces noodles
1 pound cheddar cheese, grated
1 large can tomatoes

Brown hamburger, sausage, and onion in skillet. Cook noodles in salted water until tender; drain. Layer meat mixture, noodles, cheese, and tomatoes in 9x13-inch baking dish. Bake at 350 degrees for 1 hour.

Serves about 8.

MEAT LOAF

2 pounds lean ground beef
½ cup each celery and parsley,
  finely chopped
1½ cups canned tomatoes
2 teaspoons grated onion
½ teaspoon salt
¼ teaspoon pepper
½ teaspoon oregano
2 teaspoons Worchestershire sauce
2 eggs, slightly beaten
1½ cups bread crumbs

Combine beef, vegetables, herbs, and seasoning in a large bowl. Mix well. Add eggs, then bread crumbs. Shape into loaf and place in oven cooking bag. Bake for 1 hour at 350 degrees.

Serves 6 to 8.

About the only leftover June and John would eat was a ham or meat loaf sandwich. One of their favorite meals was meat loaf, pinto beans, and cornbread.

CARRIE CASH'S MEAT LOAF FOR TWO

1 pound ground beef
½ cup crackers, crumbled
1½ teaspoons onion salt
1 dash pepper
2 teaspoons brown sugar
1 egg
½ cup milk
3 teaspoons soy sauce
Chopped onion and sweet pepper to taste

Mix all ingredients and form loaf. Bake in a 12x8-inch baking dish at 350 degrees for 1 hour.

J ohn's mother, Carrie Cash, gave me this recipe.

OYSTER STEW

1 pint oysters
1 stick butter
1 large can evaporated milk
1 tablespoon fresh parsley, chopped
½ cup onion, chopped
1 quart milk
1 teaspoon Worchestershire sauce
Salt and black pepper to taste
½ cup oyster juice

Drain oysters and save juice. Sauté onions and oysters in butter until oyster edges curl. Mix remaining ingredients and heat slowly. DO NOT BOIL.

One time the Spences, good friends of June and John, brought us some shrimp and oysters from Florida. Donna cooked them for Robert Duvall, who happened to be visiting us at the time.

FRIED PORK CHOPS

4 to 6 center cut-pork chops
Flour
Salt
Pepper
Wesson or Mazola oil

Wash pork chops and pat dry. Salt and pepper each side. Roll in flour until coated on both sides. Pour oil about ¼ inch deep in regular skillet (not iron) and heat. Cook slowly on medium heat until brown on both sides.

Make gravy same as chicken gravy. (See page 86.)

John and June weren't big meat eaters, but pork chops was one of their favorite dishes.

PORK CHOP AND POTATO CASSEROLE

6 to 8 medium pork chops
Wesson or Mazola oil
Tony Chachere's Creole Seasoning
6 to 8 potatoes, sliced
1 large onion
1 can mushroom soup
1 can water
Salt and pepper to taste
1 small can mushrooms

Coat pork chops with seasoning and pan fry in small amount of oil. Arrange chops in bottom of 9x13-inch baking dish. Layer sliced potatoes and onions over pork chops. Mix soup and water; pour over dish. Top with mushrooms, cover. Bake at 350 degrees for 30 to 45 minutes or until done.

PORK ROAST

2- to 3-pound pork tenderloin roast
4 potatoes
Salt and pepper

Line baking pan with aluminum foil, long enough to fold over top of roast. Peel potatoes. Rub roast with salt and pepper; place in baking pan with potatoes on either side. Fold foil over top. Bake at 350 degrees until well done but not dry, about 1 hour.

JUNE'S POT ROAST

June taught me to make pot roast in an oven cooking bag. It never fails and the roast is always moist and tender. If there was any roast left over, I put it in vegetable soup.

3- to 4-pound rump, chuck, or
*   round roast, about 4 inches thick*
Flour
1½ teaspoons salt
Freshly ground pepper
2 bay leaves, crumbled
2 medium onions, quartered
½ cup water (or canned beef broth,
*   tomato juice, or dry red wine)*
Oven cooking bag

Trim excess fat from outside of roast and rub meat with flour, salt, and pepper. Put oven cooking bag in pan and place roast in bag. Add onions and bay leaves, then liquid. Close the bag and cook in preheated 325-degree oven 2½ to 3 hours. Test for tenderness by piercing through bag with a fork.

Either I helped June in the kitchen or she helped me.

QUESADILLAS

One time on the bus I was making quesadillas for lunch. I was getting ready to turn them, when June said she'd show me how to flip them. She showed me all right—the quesadillas ended up on the floor. June laughed and said, "That's all right. We'll just give it to Helen," her sister. We didn't tell Helen until she was done eating. June reassured her by saying "Honey, it's fine. The skillet was so hot, it killed all the germs."

Flour tortillas
1 onion, thinly sliced
1 red bell pepper, chopped
1 green bell pepper, chopped
Cheddar cheese

On each tortilla, spread in layers onions, bell peppers, and cheese. Fold in half. Lightly grease a skillet and brown on one side. Carefully flip and brown on other side.

*June's daughter Carlene, right, joins her aunt
Helen Carter and her mom on stage.*

ROAST TURKEY

Whole turkey
1 stick butter
Salt
Pepper
Garlic powder
Melted butter

We had a big Thanksgiving dinner at the house in Hendersonville for all of June's and John's children and grandchildren who were close enough to come. Then we'd leave right after Thanksgiving to go to Jamaica for the winter months. When June and John started getting sick we left before Thanksgiving, starting in about 2000.

Remove giblets. Wash turkey and pat dry with paper towels. Wash neck, gizzard, and liver and stuff them inside the turkey with stick of butter. Sprinkle turkey with salt, pepper, and a little garlic powder. Place turkey on aluminum foil on rack of roasting pan. Baste with melted butter. Make tent of foil over turkey. Add a little water to roasting pan. Bake at 350 degrees about 20 minutes per pound. During last 30 minutes, open foil so turkey will brown nicely.

Remove neck, gizzard, and liver from cavity and set aside for making giblet gravy. (See page 115.) Place turkey on a serving platter and garnish with parsley. Save drippings in pan for dressing.

*June has an elegant dinner party to celebrate my
sister Shirley's birthday.*

TURKEY DRESSING

Here's a typical menu for Thanksgiving dinner with the Cash and Carter families:

- Turkey, dressing, and giblet gravy
- Fresh green beans
- Mashed potatoes
- Silver Queen corn from the freezer
- Sweet potatoes
- Cranberry sauce
- Deviled eggs
- Cornbread
- Chocolate pie
- Sweet potato pie

1 skillet Peggy's famous cornbread
   (page 10), crumbled
6 slices white bread, toasted
   and crumbled
½ cup cracker crumbs
2 tablespoons sage
1 teaspoon salt
1½ teaspoons black pepper
3 eggs, boiled and chopped
2 cups chicken broth
1 large onion, chopped
¾ cup celery, chopped
Drippings from turkey

In large bowl, combine cornbread, toast, cracker crumbs and boiled eggs. Add sage, salt, and pepper and mix well. Set aside.

Add onion and celery to chicken broth and cook until tender. Add turkey drippings. Pour over bread mixture, and mix well. Bake in a greased 11x14-inch pan or dish in a preheated 400-degree oven until golden brown on top.

GIBLET GRAVY

½ cup chopped onion
½ cup chopped celery
2 tablespoons self-rising flour
4 tablespoons water
2 cups broth
4 tablespoons butter
2 eggs, boiled and chopped
Neck, liver, and gizzard cooked inside
*   turkey, chopped*

Sauté onions and celery. Make paste of flour and water and stir slowly into broth. Cook and stir until well blended. Add butter, eggs, onion, celery, giblets, salt, and pepper. Simmer until thick. Serve over dressing.

SAUSAGE PINWHEELS

1 pound sausage
Biscuit dough (see page 4)

Make Peggy's homemade biscuit dough. (See page 4.) On floured board or wax paper, roll out ⅓ of dough in rectangle. Spread uncooked sausage evenly over dough. Roll up jelly-roll fashion, securing ends. Repeat with rest of dough and sausage. Slice rolls ¼- to ½-inch thick. Place on cookie sheet and bake at 400 degrees until brown, about 15 minutes.

The Statler Brothers, who appeared with John as far back as the Sixties, came to visit us often. They really liked these sausage pinwheels, which I served as part of a light breakfast.

SEAFOOD AU GRATIN

½ pound butter or margarine
3 stalks celery, grated
1 large onion, chopped
3 green onions, chopped
5 tablespoons flour
1½ large cans evaporated milk
8 ounces mozzarella cheese, grated
8 ounces cheddar cheese, grated
2 egg yolks
1 pound crab meat
1 pound shrimp

Sauté onions and celery in butter. Add flour and blend. Add milk. Remove from heat. Add all but ¼ cup each of cheese, egg yolks, crab meat, and shrimp. Pour into greased 9x12-inch casserole dish. Sprinkle remaining ½ cup cheese on top. Bake at 350 degrees for 30 minutes.

Backstage at the Opry are June, Robert Duvall,
Connie Smith, and Anita Carter.

BETTY'S FRIED FISH

Fish (½ pound per person)
Lemon pepper
Self-rising cornmeal
Mazola or Crisco oil

John loved fried fish, especially if my sister Betty did the frying. He thought her fish was the absolute best. Sometimes when we'd go check on him while he was spending a few days by himself at the farm in Bon Aqua, Betty would fry up any fish he had caught.

Cut fish into small pieces. Wash well in cold water and pat dry with paper towels Heat oil in deep fat fryer according to manufacturer's directions. Sprinkle fish with lemon pepper. Roll in self-rising cornmeal. Place fish in hot oil and fry until golden brown, turning as needed, about 5 minutes. Drain on paper towels.

NOTE: You can use heavy iron skillet instead of deep fat fryer. Pour Mazola or Crisco oil in skillet until it is about one inch deep and heat until hot but not smoking. Place fish in hot oil and fry 2 to 3 minutes until bottom is golden brown. Turn carefully and brown other side. Drain on paper towels.

I caught this big fellow and cooked it for dinner.

COUNTRY FRIED STEAK

2-pound round steak
½ cup all-purpose flour
1 teaspoon salt
¼ teaspoon pepper
½ cup vegetable oil

Cut steak into 8 serving pieces. Combine the flour, salt, and pepper; coat the steaks on both sides with flour mixture. In a heavy skillet, heat the oil and sauté the steaks for 5 minutes on each side or until tender. Remove the steaks to a serving platter, reserving 4 tablespoons of the pan juices. Serve with Pan Gravy.

Makes 8 servings.

PAN GRAVY

3 tablespoons all-purpose flour
4 tablespoons pan juices
2¼ cups milk
1 teaspoon salt
¼ teaspoon pepper

Blend flour into reserved pan juices in skillet, stirring constantly until smooth and bubbly. Remove from heat. Stir in milk, salt, and pepper. Continue cooking, stirring and scraping browned bits from bottom and sides of skillet until gravy thickens and bubbles, about 1 minute. Be sure to keep gravy medium brown.

I never knew how many people would be eating with us when it came time to sit down at the table. Whoever was visiting was invited to join us for lunch or supper. I just added to what I was cooking—either more of the same or another dish—and we always seemed to have enough.

Cakes

ANGEL FOOD CAKE

1 cup sifted cake flour
½ cup sugar
Whites of 12 eggs
1½ teaspoons cream of tartar
¼ teaspoon salt
1 teaspoon vanilla extract
¼ teaspoon almond extract
1 cup sugar

Sift the flour and ½ cup sugar onto wax paper. Sift this mixture three times to make it light. Beat egg whites until frothy. Add cream of tartar, salt, vanilla, and almond extract. Beat until peaks form. Add 1 cup sugar, one tablespoon at a time; continue beating until stiff peaks form. Fold flour mixture, ¼ cup at a time, into the egg whites. Put batter in an ungreased 10-inch tube pan. Using a knife, cut through the batter several times to remove air pockets. Bake at 375 degrees, about 35 minutes, until cake springs back when touched, or a wooden toothpick inserted halfway between the center and edge comes out clean.

June was the sweet eater. We both collected recipes and made cakes real often.

SNOWBALL CAKE

1 box angel food cake mix
2 containers Cool Whip
2 packages unflavored gelatin
1 cup sugar
1 cup boiling water
½ cup cold water
No. 2 can crushed pineapple, drained
2 tablespoons lemon juice
Shredded coconut

Bake cake according to directions on package.

Mix sugar, gelatin, and boiling water until the gelatin dissolves. Add cold water, pineapple, lemon juice, pineapple juice, and one container of Cool Whip; stir well. Break the cake into little pieces. Alternate layers of cake and pineapple mixture in a 10-inch tube pan. Refrigerate for three hours or overnight.

Turn the cake onto a serving plate and spread the remaining container of Cool Whip over the top. Sprinkle with coconut.

CARROT CAKE

2 cups all-purpose flour, sifted

2 teaspoons baking powder

1 teaspoon soda

1 teaspoon salt

1 teaspoon cinnamon

1⅓ cups canola oil

2 cups sugar

4 eggs

3 cups grated carrots

1½ cups pecans

1 medium-sized can crushed pineapple

Sift dry ingredients together. Combine oil and sugar. Beat in flour mixture, alternating with eggs. Stir in carrots, drained pineapple, and pecans. Pour into lightly oiled 10-inch tube pan. Bake at 300 degrees for 1 hour or until knife comes clean when inserted in cake. DO NOT OVERBAKE.

CARROT-NUT CAKE

2 cups all-purpose flour
1¾ cups sugar
1 teaspoon salt
1 teaspoon baking soda
1 teaspoon baking powder
2 teaspoons cinnamon
1½ cups Wesson oil
4 eggs
3 cups shredded carrots
⅔ cup chopped nuts
1 teaspoon vanilla extract

Preheat oven to 350 degrees.

Sift together flour, sugar, salt, baking soda, baking powder, and cinnamon in mixing bowl. Add oil; mix well. Add eggs; blend thoroughly. Add carrots; mix well. Stir in nuts and vanilla extract. Pour the batter into 9x13-inch greased and floured pan. Bake 30 minutes. Spread Cream Cheese Icing (next page) on cooled cake.

CREAM CHEESE ICING

4 tablespoons (½ stick) butter
8-ounce package cream cheese, softened
1-pound box confectioners sugar
1 teaspoon vanilla extract
⅔ cup chopped nuts

Cream butter and cream cheese. Mix in sugar, then vanilla and nuts. Spread on cooled cake.

EASY CHEESE CAKE

8 ounces sour cream
8 ounces cream cheese
8 ounces Cool Whip
⅓ cup sugar
2 teaspoons vanilla
1 graham cracker crust

June's favorite dessert was any kind of cheesecake. I went nearly every day to the Wyndham Hotel near our house in Jamaica to buy one or two of its famous cheesecakes. I went so often the baker asked me what in the world we were doing with so many cheesecakes and if we were selling them.

Gradually beat in sugar with cream cheese. Add vanilla, sour cream, and Cool Chip. Blend well. Spoon mixture into graham cracker crust. Chill in refrigerator until firm. Garnish with favorite fruit filling.

Cakes

COCONUT CAKE

1 cup butter

2 cups sugar

5 eggs

1 teaspoon soda

Dash of salt

2¾ cups cake flour

1 teaspoon baking powder

1 cup buttermilk

1 teaspoon vanilla extract

½ to ¾ teaspoon coconut extract

2 cups fresh grated coconut (save 1 cup
*   to put on top of cake)*

½ cup milk

½ cup sugar

John wasn't much on eating sweets, but my coconut cake was his favorite. When I made this cake during the Christmas holidays, I'd decorate it with candy canes or large gum drops.

Cream butter and sugar until smooth. Add eggs, beating after each addition. Sift dry ingredients. Add to creamed mixture, alternating with buttermilk. Stir in flavorings. Bake in three or four greased and floured 9-inch round pans. Bake at 350 degrees for 25 minutes. Cool.

Before icing cake, boil 1 cup grated coconut with milk and sugar. Poke holes in layers and drizzle over layers as you assemble. Frost with Seven-Minute Icing (next page) and cover top and sides with remaining coconut.

SEVEN-MINUTE ICING

2 unbeaten egg whites
1½ cups sugar
⅓ cup water
1½ tablespoons light corn syrup
1 teaspoon vanilla

Combine all ingredients except vanilla. Put in double boiler. Place over boiling water. While water is boiling, beat with electric mixer 7 minutes or more until frosting stands in peaks. Remove from water, add vanilla, and beat until thick enough to spread.

Double recipe for more than 2 9-inch layers.

JUNE'S BLACKBERRY JAM CAKE

4 cups flour
2 teaspoons cinnamon
2 teaspoons nutmeg
1 teaspoon cloves
1½ teaspoons allspice
¼ teaspoon salt
1½ cup butter
2 cups sugar
6 egg yolks, well beaten
1 cup buttermilk
*1½ teaspoons soda dissolved
   in buttermilk*
2 cups blackberry jam
6 egg whites (well beaten)

We didn't have as many sweets like June's special blackberry jam cake around the house after John was diagnosed with diabetes. We had to watch him like a kid to keep him from sneaking bites of whatever dessert we had.

Sift flour, cinnamon, nutmeg, cloves, allspice, and salt twice. Set aside. Cream butter and sugar; then add beaten egg yolks and buttermilk with soda. Stir in dry mixture. Add blackberry jam. Fold in 6 egg whites. Pour into four 9-inch round cake pans. Bake in 375-degree oven for about 30 minutes.

BLACKBERY JAM CAKE ICING

2 cups sugar
1 cup milk
½ cup butter

In saucepan bring sugar, milk, and butter to boil; cook over moderate heat for 10 minutes. Spread hot sauce on the warm layers. This will appear runny but when it cools, the icing will set and be firm.

KATHY CASH'S FOUR-LAYER COCONUT CAKE

Duncan Hines butter recipe yellow cake mix
1 cup granulated sugar
1 cup confectioners sugar
2 12-ounce packages fresh frozen coconut
3 cups Cool Whip

When Jimmy and I first married, his sister Mary Bloodworth made this cake. I got the recipe from her and now it's part of our tradition every Thanksgiving and Christmas.

Kathy Cash Tittle

Mix and bake the cake mix as directed on box. Place in two greased round 9-inch pans. While the cake is baking, blend the sugars, sour cream, and one 12-ounce package of coconut. After the cake cools, slice each layer in half to make four layers Spread all but one cup of the sugar/sour cream/coconut mixture between the three layers; stack as you go. Blend the reserved cup of mixture with Cool Whip and frost the top and sides of cake. Sprinkle the top and sides of the cake with the other package of coconut. To get the coconut to stay on the sides of the cake, hold one hand almost touching the cake while you sprinkle.

Refrigerate in airtight plastic cake container at least 2 to 3 days before serving.

This cake can also be frozen if you want to make it ahead of time. Just thaw it in refrigerator at least 2 or 3 days before serving.

JUNE'S MILLION-DOLLAR POUND CAKE

3 cups sugar

4 cups flour

1 teaspoon baking powder

1 teaspoon almond extract

1 pound butter, softened

¾ cup milk

6 eggs at room temperature

Mix together all dry ingredients. Add softened butter, flavoring and milk. Add eggs one at a time, beating after each. Bake in 10-inch greased and floured tube pan at 300 degrees for approximately 1 hour and 40 minutes or until done.

I have never had a failure making this cake from June's recipe. I don't watch it or open the oven door until the time is up.

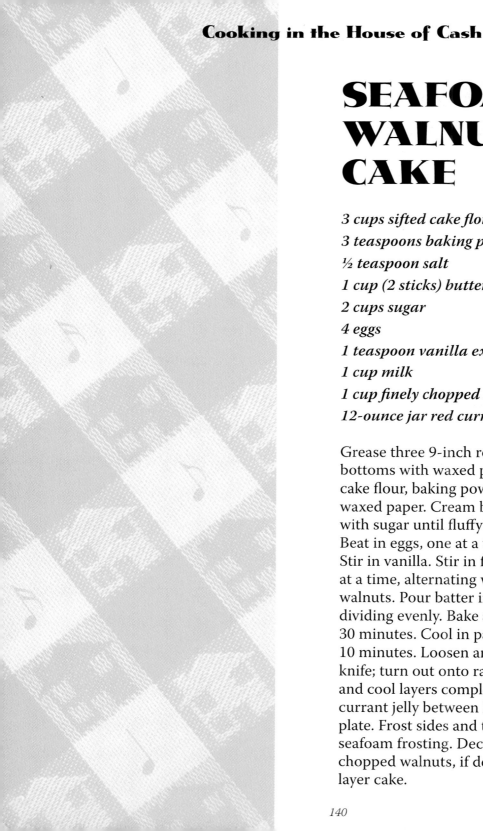

SEAFOAM WALNUT CAKE

3 cups sifted cake flour

3 teaspoons baking powder

½ teaspoon salt

1 cup (2 sticks) butter or margarine

2 cups sugar

4 eggs

1 teaspoon vanilla extract

1 cup milk

1 cup finely chopped black walnuts

12-ounce jar red currant jelly

Grease three 9-inch round cake pans; line bottoms with waxed paper and grease. Sift cake flour, baking powder, and salt onto waxed paper. Cream butter or margarine with sugar until fluffy in a large bowl. Beat in eggs, one at a time, until fluffy. Stir in vanilla. Stir in flour mixture, a third at a time, alternating with milk. Fold in walnuts. Pour batter into prepared pans, dividing evenly. Bake at 375 degrees for 30 minutes. Cool in pans on wire racks 10 minutes. Loosen around edges with a knife; turn out onto racks. Peel off paper and cool layers completely. Spread with currant jelly between layers on a serving plate. Frost sides and top of cake with seafoam frosting. Decorate with additional chopped walnuts, if desired. Makes triple-layer cake.

SEAFOAM FROSTING

1½ cups brown sugar, firmly packed
¼ cup water
2 egg whites, unbeaten
2 tablespoons light corn syrup
¼ teaspoon salt
¼ teaspoon salt
1 teaspoon vanilla extract

Combine all ingredients in the top of a
double boiler and beat until blended. Place
over simmering water. Cook, beating
constantly with an electric or rotary beater
for 5 minutes or until mixture triples in
volume and holds firm marks of beater.
Remove from heat. Makes enough to frost
triple-layer cake.

SOCK-IT-TO-ME CAKE

1 pound (4 sticks) butter, softened
1 box yellow cake mix
8-ounce container sour cream
⅔ cup oil
½ cup granulated sugar
4 eggs
1 cup chopped nuts
1 teaspoon vanilla extract
1 teaspoon cinnamon
2 teaspoons brown sugar

This is an excellent coffee cake for breakfast or a mid-morning snack.

Thoroughly mix all ingredients except cinnamon and brown sugar. Pour half the batter into a bundt pan. Mix together the cinnamon and brown sugar; sprinkle over the batter in the pan. Pour the other half of the batter over the cinnamon and sugar. Bake in a preheated oven at 350 degrees for 1 hour.

VANILLA WAFER CAKE

2 cups granulated sugar
2 sticks butter (margarine can be used
    but butter is better)
6 large eggs
16-ounce box vanilla wafers, crushed
2 cups coconut
2 cups chopped pecans

Cream butter and sugar together. Add eggs one at a time and mix well. Add vanilla wafers slowly to mixture. Add nuts and coconut and mix until well blended. The batter will be very thick. Place in a greased and floured tube pan. Bake at 300 degrees for 1½ hours or until inserted knife comes out clean. Let cool and frost with cream cheese frosting. (See page 144.)

This cake is delicious. It's really rich so only small slices are needed for a great dessert. It's also good with ice cream. This is another recipe given to us by Leanne Abell, one of June and John's nurses at Baptist Hospital.

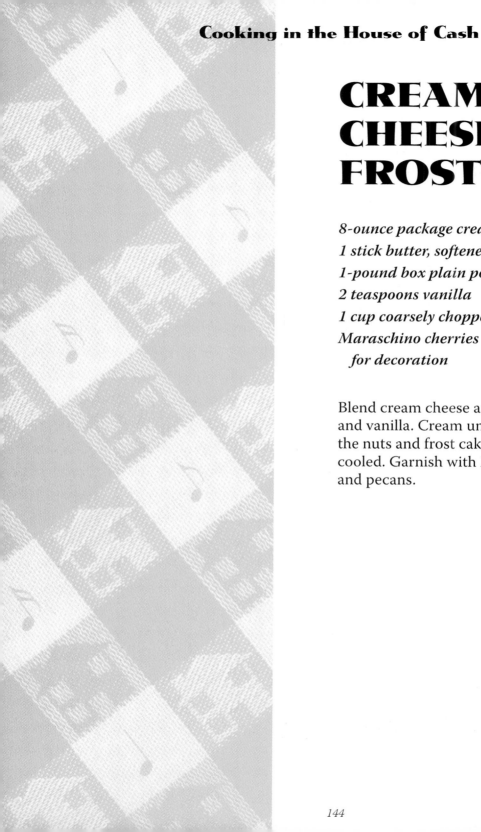

CREAM CHEESE FROSTING

8-ounce package cream cheese
1 stick butter, softened
1-pound box plain powdered sugar
2 teaspoons vanilla
1 cup coarsely chopped pecans
Maraschino cherries and pecan halves
  for decoration

Blend cream cheese and butter. Add sugar and vanilla. Cream until smooth. Fold in the nuts and frost cake as soon as it has cooled. Garnish with Maraschino cherries and pecans.

Johnny and his great fan Dennis Devine in 1967

Pies

BUTTERMILK PIE

3 eggs, beaten
1 cup sugar
1 tablespoon flour
1 cup buttermilk
1 tablespoon butter, melted
1 teaspoon vanilla extract
1 pie shell, unbaked

Combine eggs with sugar and flour. Add buttermilk, butter, and vanilla. Mix well. Pour into pastry shell and bake at 350 degrees for 40 to 45 minutes.

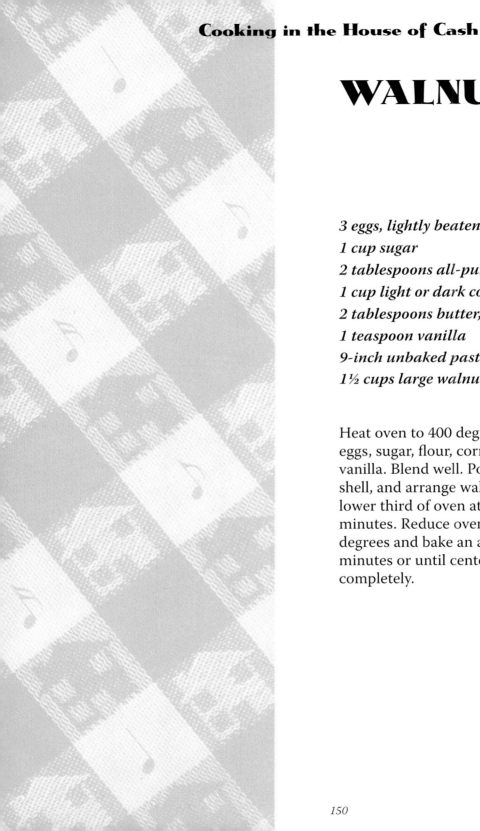

WALNUT PIE

3 eggs, lightly beaten
1 cup sugar
2 tablespoons all-purpose flour
1 cup light or dark corn syrup
2 tablespoons butter, melted
1 teaspoon vanilla
9-inch unbaked pastry pie shell
1½ cups large walnuts

Heat oven to 400 degrees. Combine eggs, sugar, flour, corn syrup, butter, and vanilla. Blend well. Pour into unbaked pie shell, and arrange walnuts on top. Bake in lower third of oven at 400 degrees for 15 minutes. Reduce oven temperature to 350 degrees and bake an additional 35 to 45 minutes or until center appears set. Cool completely.

CHESS PIE

1 cup sugar
1 tablespoon cornmeal
½ stick butter, melted
3 eggs, beaten
1 tablespoon vinegar
1 tablespoon vanilla extract
⅓ cup whole milk
1 unbaked pie shell

Mix sugar and corn meal together, set aside. Combine eggs, milk, vanilla, and butter and add to sugar mixture. Mix well, add vinegar, pour into pie shell. Bake at 400 degrees for 10 minutes, then reduce heat to 325 and bake for 20 to 25 minutes until golden brown on top. Remove and let cool.

Nobody knows for sure how this Southern pie got its name. One story is that it kept well in a pie chest, a cupboard where pies were stored a century ago. Chest pie then became just chess. The other is when asked what kind of pie she'd baked, the cook said she didn't know. "It's jes' pie."

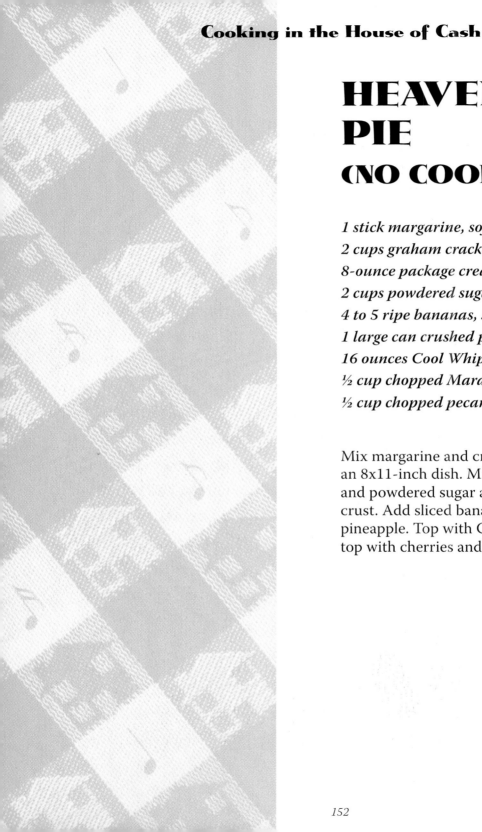

HEAVENLY PIE
(NO COOKING)

1 stick margarine, softened
2 cups graham cracker crumbs
8-ounce package cream cheese, softened
2 cups powdered sugar
4 to 5 ripe bananas, sliced
1 large can crushed pineapple, drained
16 ounces Cool Whip
½ cup chopped Maraschino cherries
½ cup chopped pecans

Mix margarine and crumbs. Press into an 8x11-inch dish. Mix cream cheese and powdered sugar and spread over crust. Add sliced bananas then crushed pineapple. Top with Cool Whip. Sprinkle top with cherries and pecans.

Pies

John's Favorite
CHOCOLATE
PIE

4 heaping tablespoons flour

4 rounded tablespoons cocoa

1 cup sugar

3 egg yolks

1 cup milk

1 cup cold water

½ stick butter

1 pie shell, baked

Cool Whip or whipped cream

Thanksgiving was a two-dessert day. I made sweet potato pie, June's favorite, as well as a chocolate pie for John.

Put flour, cocoa, and sugar in heavy sauce pan and mix well. Beat egg yolks with milk, water and melted butter and add to sauce pan. Cook over medium heat, stirring constantly until thick. Pour into prepared pie shell. Refrigerate.

Serve plain or with Cool Whip or whipped cream.

June's Favorite SWEET POTATO PIE

1 pound sweet potatoes, diced and cooked
3 eggs
½ cup firmly packed dark brown sugar
½ teaspoon salt
½ teaspoon ground cinnamon
¼ teaspoon ground nutmeg
⅛ teaspoon ground ginger
1 dash of ground allspice
1 tall can evaporated milk
1 cup whipping cream
1 tablespoon molasses
Rich pastry shell

Pare sweet potatoes and dice. Cook, covered, in boiling slightly salted water in a medium-size saucepan 15 minutes or until tender. Drain, shake in pan over low heat to dry. Mash, then beat until smooth with an electric beater.

Beat eggs slightly in a large bowl. Stir in brown sugar, salt, spices, sweet potatoes, and milk. Pour into chilled pastry shell. (See next page.)

Bake in hot oven at 425 degrees for 5 minutes; then lower oven temperature to 325 degrees and bake for 40 minutes, or until center is almost set but still soft. (Do not overbake, for custard will set as it cools.) Cool pie on a wire rack.

When ready to serve, mix whipping cream and molasses in a medium-sized bowl. Beat until stiff. Spoon onto pie.

John enjoys a slice of watermelon during one of his last visits to June's homeplace in Virginia.

RICH PASTRY

1½ cups all-purpose flour
½ teaspoon salt
¼ cup shortening
4 tablespoons butter or margerine
4 tablespoons cold water

Combine 1½ cups sifted all-purpose flour and ½ teaspoon salt in a large bowl; cut in ¼ cup shortening and 4 tablespoons (½ stick) butter or margarine with a pastry blender until mixture is crumbly. Sprinkle with 4 tablespoons cold water, 1 tablespoon at a time. Mix lightly with a fork just until pastry holds together and leaves side of bowl clean.

Roll out pastry to a 12-inch round on a lightly floured pastry cloth or board. Fit into a 9-inch pie plate. Trim overhang to ½ inch, turn under flush with rim. (Flute to make a stand-up edge.) Chill while making filling for filled pies, then bake according to baking instructions.

For unfilled pies, prick pastry with a fork and bake at 425 degrees until brown, about 10 to 15 minutes.

Cookies and Puddings

BANANA PUDDING

1 large box instant vanilla pudding mix
3 cups milk
1 box vanilla wafers
5 to 6 bananas
8 ounces Cool Whip

Mix vanilla pudding with milk according to directions and set aside. (Note: the mixture will not get thick.) Place half of box of wafers in 8x11-inch dish. Slice enough bananas to cover the wafers. Repeat layers of wafers and bananas. Pour pudding mixture over the entire dish. Top with Cool Whip.

I made a lot of banana puddings in Jamaica. We had a banana tree in our yard so I'd pull off a whole stalk and hang it from the ceiling. All I had to do was reach up and grab bananas for a pudding, fruit salad, or a snack.

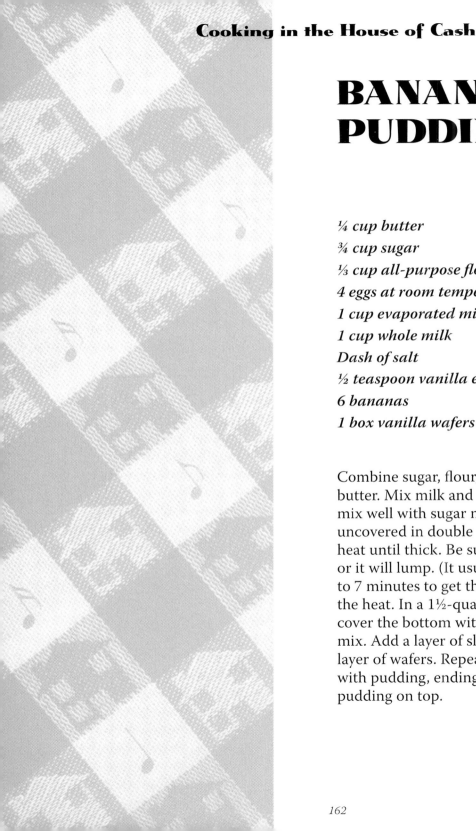

BANANA PUDDING

¼ cup butter

¾ cup sugar

⅓ cup all-purpose flour

4 eggs at room temperature, separated

1 cup evaporated milk

1 cup whole milk

Dash of salt

½ teaspoon vanilla extract

6 bananas

1 box vanilla wafers

Combine sugar, flour, and salt. Cream with butter. Mix milk and egg yolks together; mix well with sugar mixture. Cook uncovered in double boiler on medium heat until thick. Be sure to stir constantly or it will lump. (It usually takes about 5 to 7 minutes to get thick.) Remove from the heat. In a 1½-quart glass baking bowl, cover the bottom with some of pudding mix. Add a layer of sliced bananas and layer of wafers. Repeat layers beginning with pudding, ending with a thin layer of pudding on top.

MERINGUE

6 tablespoons sugar
4 egg whites
¼ teaspoon cream of tartar

In a large bowl, beat egg whites and cream of tartar with electric mixer on medium speed until foamy. Gradually add the sugar to egg white mixture. Beat on high until stiff peaks form. Spoon on top of the pudding mixture, making it peak. Bake at 425 for about 5 minutes. Remove from oven and let cool or chill before serving.

JOHN'S CHERRY DELIGHT

16-ounce can crushed pineapple
16-ounce can cherry pie filling
8 tablespoons (1 stick) butter
1 box white cake mix
1 cup chopped pecans

Donna Spence gave me this recipe. She and her husband Joe, a minister, were good friends of June and John. It's real easy to make and very good— and one of John's favorites.

Butter a large, 2-inch deep oblong baking pan. Layer bottom of the pan with the crushed pineapple; spread the cherry pie filling over the pineapple. Cut the butter into the cake mix until the mixture is crumbly; sprinkle the cake mix over the pineapple and pie filling. Sprinkle the nuts over the top of the cake mix. Bake at 350 degrees about 40 minutes.

PEGGY'S CHERRIED TREASURE

2 sticks butter
2 cups flour
4 tablespoons granulated sugar
1½ cups pecans, chopped
8-ounce package cream cheese
16-ounce box powdered sugar
1 large container Cool Whip
1 can cherry pie filling

This is another dessert we had to keep away from John, who wasn't supposed to eat sweets because of his diabetes.

Melt butter in 8x12-inch baking dish. Add flour, granulated sugar, and nuts. Mix well and pat in dish to form crust. Bake at 350 degrees till light brown.

Cream together cream cheese and powdered sugar. Fold Cool Whip into mixture. Spread on cooled crust. Top with cherry pie filling.

PEACH COBBLER

1 large can peaches (undrained)
½ cup water
1 cup sugar
1¼ cups flour
1 stick butter
1 tablespoon vanilla extract

Place peaches in 8x12-inch baking dish. Add ½ cup water. Sprinkle vanilla over peaches. Place sugar, butter, and flour in mixing bowl. Work these three ingredients until mixture becomes crumbly. Sprinkle over peaches. Bake at 375 degrees until light brown. Serve with ice cream or Cool Whip.

This isn't an old-fashioned cobbler made with fresh peaches, but it's mighty good. You can make this one any time of the year.

CREAM CHEESE DAINTY COOKIES

½ cup butter, creamed
3-ounce package cream cheese
½ cup granulated sugar
1 cup self-rising flour
2 teaspoons baking powder
½ teaspoon salt
½ teaspoon almond extract
Crushed wheat flakes
Maraschino cherries

These light cookies are very delectable and are wonderful with a cup of hot tea.

Cream butter and cream cheese to a soft consistency. Mix in sugar. Add flour, salt, and baking powder. Mix well and then add almond extract. Chill the dough for 1 hour. Roll into small balls, and then roll in the crushed wheat flakes. Place on lightly greased cookie sheet and lightly flatten with a fork. Place half of a Maraschino cherry in the center. Bake at 350 degrees for 15 minutes. The cookies do not brown.

BROWNIES

1 cup butter (2 sticks)

2 cups sugar

4 eggs

6 tablespoons unsweetened cocoa

2 teaspoons vanilla extract

1 cup all-purpose flour

Preheat oven to 325 degrees. Grease
9x13-inch pan. Cream butter and sugar.
Add eggs, cocoa, and vanilla; beat until
smooth. Mix in flour. Spread batter in
prepared pan. Bake 25 to 30 minutes. Cool
and cut into squares.

JUNE'S HELLO DOLLIES

1 stick butter
1 cup graham cracker crumbs
1 cup chocolate chips
1 cup coconut
1 cup pecans
1 can condensed milk

These bar cookies, one of June's recipes, are easy to make. June and I often wondered where the name came from.

Melt butter in a 13x9-inch baking pan. Spread graham cracker crumbs over bottom of baking pan. Layer chocolate chips, coconut, and pecans over crumbs. Pour milk over the layers. Bake in a 350-degree oven for 30 minutes.

ORANGE SUGAR SQUARES

2½ cups all-purpose flour, sifted
2 teaspoons baking powder
1 teaspoon salt
¾ cup (1½ sticks) butter or margarine
1½ cups sugar
2 eggs
1 tablespoon grated orange rind

Measure flour, baking powder, and salt into sifter. Cream butter or margarine with one cup of the sugar until fluffy in a large bowl. Beat in eggs and orange rind. Sift in flour mixture, a third at a time, blending well. Chill until firm enough to handle. Roll out dough to a 16-inch square on a lightly floured pastry cloth or board. Sprinkle with remaining ¼ cup sugar. Cut into 4-inch squares. Place one inch apart on large cookie sheet. Bake at 400 degrees for 8 minutes or until firm. Remove cookies to wire rack to cool. Leave plain or drizzle with your favorite orange frosting.

June would not use paper napkins — ever. We set the table with linen tablecloths and napkins, sterling silver, fine china, and crystal for dinner whether we were in Hendersonville, Florida, or Jamaica. Even the TV trays—on the rare occasions we used them—had linen placemats and napkins.

MAYBELLE'S OLD-FASHIONED TEA CAKES

2 sticks margarine
2 cups sugar
2 eggs
3 cups all-purpose flour
2½ teaspoons baking powder
1 dash salt
1 tablespoon vanilla extract

Mix all ingredients together. Roll out on lightly floured board and cut with cookie cutter. (I use the top of a glass.) Place on greased cookie sheet and bake at 350 degrees 15 minutes.

Makes about 50 cookies.

Maybelle gave me this recipe. I hadn't cooked too much when I started staying with her and Mr. Carter. She taught me a lot about cooking and about life.

Maybelle and I visit with Aunt Mary Bays, Sarah Carter's mother-in-law, who lived to be 110.

OATMEAL ICEBOX COOKIES

1 cup shortening
1 cup brown sugar
1 cup white sugar
2 eggs
1 teaspoon vanilla extract
1½ cups all-purpose flour, sifted
1 teaspoon baking soda
1 teaspoon salt
3 cups quick-cooking oats

Over the years June collected a lot of recipes from family members and friends. She was a good cook, and we had many fun times in the kitchen.

Cream shortening with brown and white sugars. Add eggs and vanilla. Beat well. Add flour sifted with soda and salt.

Stir in oats. Shape in four rolls on waxed paper. Chill in refrigerator several hours. Cut in thin slices, about ¼-inch thick.

Bake on cookie sheet at 300 degrees about 15 minutes.

PRALINE COOKIES

*1 package (⅓ box) Keebler Honey
Graham crackers*
2 sticks butter
½ cup sugar
½ cup chopped nuts

Break crackers into sections. Place flat on cookie sheet letting sides of crackers touch. Melt butter. Add sugar and bring to a boil. Boil three minutes stirring constantly. Add nuts and pour over crackers. Place in 325-degree oven for 12 minutes. Remove from pan immediately, separating cracker sections, and place on foil to cool. May be frozen.

These are so good, you'd never guess they're made with graham crackers.

MARSH-MALLOW FUDGE

4 ounces unsweetened chocolate

2 tablespoons margarine

½ cup light corn syrup

2 tablespoons water

1 teaspoon vanilla extract

16-ounce box confectioners sugar

⅓ cup dry milk

1 cup miniature marshmallows

Melt chocolate and margarine over low heat. Stir in corn syrup, water, vanilla, sugar, and dry milk. Fold in one cup miniature marshmallows. Spread in greased 8-inch pan. Chill two hours.

FAST 'N FABULOUS DARK CHOCOLATE FUDGE

½ cup light or dark corn syrup

⅓ cup evaporated milk

*3 cups (18 ounces) semisweet
  chocolate chips*

¾ cup confectioners sugar, sifted

2 teaspoons vanilla

1½ cups coarsely chopped walnuts

Line 8-inch square baking pan with plastic
wrap. In 3-quart microwaveable bowl,
combine corn syrup and evaporated milk,
stirring until well blended. Microwave on
high. Stir in chocolate chips until melted.
Stir in confectioners sugar, vanilla, and
walnuts. With wooden spoon, beat until
thick and glossy. Spread in prepared pan.
Refrigerate two hours or until firm.

Makes 25 squares.

MAYBELLE'S PEANUT BRITTLE

5 cups sugar
1 cup white syrup
1 cup water
2 cups peanuts
2 tablespoons (¼ stick) butter
2 pinches of salt
2 teaspoons baking soda

In a heavy saucepan, combine the sugar, syrup, and water; cook until almost at hard ball stage. Add the peanuts; cook until hard and golden. Remove from heat. Beat in the butter, salt, and baking soda. Spread thin on a greased baking sheet. Cool. Break into pieces.

This is another one of Maybelle's recipes. One time we were making some and Maybelle's brother Toob decided to help by adding the baking soda. He put in too much, and it fizzed up and ran out of the pan, spreading all over the top of the stove. It came off in one thin sheet that showed the imprint of the eyes of the stove!

This and That

RIPE TOMATO RELISH

12 onions, diced

2 bunches celery, diced

2 green peppers, diced

1 red pepper, diced

1 peck (8 quarts or ¼ bushel) ripe
tomatoes, diced

1 cup salt

1 quart vinegar

6 cups sugar

1 tablespoon cinnamon

1 tablespoon cloves

1 tablespoon ginger

1 teaspoon allspice

Combine the vegetables in a large container and add salt. Let stand overnight. Drain the vegetables. Combine the vinegar, sugar, and spices and add to the drained vegetable mixture. Bring to a boil, then pack in hot sterilized jars and seal. Turn jars on seal end until they are cool.

Jo Walker-Meador, longtime executive director of the Country Music Association, came over one night to have supper with Maybelle and me. Maybelle asked me to go down in the basement and get some chow chow, relish, and pickles for Jo to take home. When I got back, there was no Jo to be seen. When I asked Maybelle where Jo was, this little voice said, "I'm right here." She was trying to answer the telephone for Maybelle, but she tripped and was lying underneath the table.

I made this every year for June and John to eat with pinto beans and black-eyed peas.

I guess I've always known how to can, but I'm not sure many people do these days. Jars and lids should be sterilized in a pan of boiling water for 15 minutes. Wash the rubber rings in soap and hot water; rinse well and place in a pan of boiling water until ready to use. To process, place wire rack in bottom of the hot-water canner or large boiler. Fill with water to about jar height. When the water is boiling, lower the jars into the water. Jars should be about 2 inches apart and not touch the sides of the container. Add more boiling water to cover at least 1 inch above the top of the jars. Boil for 15 minutes.

GREEN TOMATO CHOW CHOW

6 large onions
12 green tomatoes (stem end removed)
12 green peppers
4 cups green beans (cut in ½-inch pieces)
4 cups cauliflower
   (broken into small buds)
4 cups fresh corn kernels
½ cup pickling salt
6 cups sugar
4 cups vinegar
2 tablespoons mustard seed
3 tablespoons celery seed
1½ teaspoons turmeric

Cut up onions, green peppers, and tomatoes and place in large bowl. Combine cut up vegetables with beans, cauliflower, and corn. Sprinkle with pickling salt and let stand overnight.

Rinse and drain vegetables. Put in large pan. Combine sugar, vinegar, mustard seed, celery seed, turmeric, and one cup water; pour over vegetables. Bring to boiling; boil gently 5 minutes. Ladle into hot jars, leaving ½-inch headspace. Adjust lids; process in boiling water for 15 minutes.

Makes 10 pints.

ROASTED PEANUTS

2 pounds raw peanuts in shell

Spread raw peanuts in shells on cookie sheet or flat pan. Roast at 350 degrees about 20 minutes, stirring every 5 minutes.

Roasted peanuts were John's favorite snack. I couldn't make a guess how many pounds of raw peanuts we roasted over the years. It seemed like we were always out.

PICKLED BEETS

10 beets, approximately
1 cup sugar
1 cup vinegar
1 sterilized quart jar

June used to string hot peppers to hang in the kitchen for decoration or use just like her mother did. She said her Daddy could eat hot pepper and never flinch.

Boil beets until soft. Skins will slip off. Peel and cut into small cubes. Put beets in large pot with sugar and vinegar. Bring to boil, stirring constantly. Put into sterilized jar and seal.

Makes 1 quart.

SQUASH PICKLES

1 gallon squash, sliced
8 small onions, diced
1 green pepper, diced
½ cup coarse salt
5 cups sugar
½ teaspoon turmeric
½ teaspoon ground cloves
2 tablespoons mustard seed
2 tablespoons celery seed
5 cups vinegar

Add salt to squash and onions; let stand in refrigerator for 1 hour. Drain and rinse mixture. Combine remaining ingredients; pour in pan and let come to a boil. Put squash, onions, and green pepper mixture in hot sterilized jars and pour boiling liquid into jars. Seal. Squash pickles will be ready to eat in about 1 week.

PEAR PRESERVES

6 cups pears, peeled and sliced
3 cups sugar

I made pear preserves from the trees in our yard at John and June's house on the lake. They were so good on a hot buttered biscuit after a big breakfast!

Place pears and sugar in heavy saucepan. Bring to a rolling boil. Turn heat down to very low. Cook for 2½ hours, stirring every 10 minutes or so, gently so pears won't break apart. Put in sterilized jars.

Makes 4 pints.

FREEZER STRAWBERRY PRESERVES

1 cup strawberries
2 cups sugar

Mix well. Let stand 20 minutes. Stir. Put in sterilized jars and keep in freezer.

Makes 2 pints.

STRAWBERRY PRESERVES

4 cups strawberries, chopped
8 cups sugar
1½ cups water, cold
2 boxes Sure Gel

Mix water and Sure Gel. Bring to a boil; boil one minute. Add to berries and stir 3 minutes. Pour into sterilized jars. Let set 24 hours. Put in freezer.

Makes 8 pints.

Index

OTHER BOOKS
by Peggy Knight

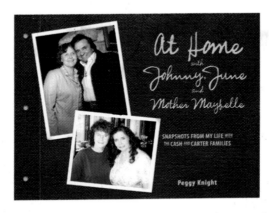

At Home with Johnny, June and Mother Maybelle
2004

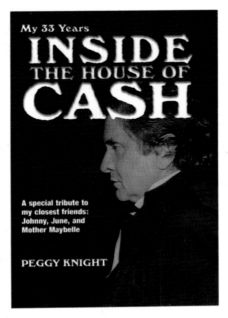

My 33 Years Inside the House of Cash
2004